Lipreadi

Here is help and reassurance for anyone confronting hearing loss for the first time. At some point after we are sixty, about a quarter of us ought to start using a hearing aid. But we won't get the best results from that alone and should combine it with lipreading. The Author is a firm advocate of lipreading classes, but for practice on our own with a mirror, with a friend or with the television, for those who can't get to classes or who want to experiment a little first, this guide to 'seeing the sound of speech' will be the greatest help.

It is organised around an outstanding series of photographs, already used on BBC Television, of the lip shapes of those sounds which can be shown as static pictures. They can often provide the key to a whole word or sentence. John Chaloner Woods explains how they can be used and built on most effectively. From his own experience learning lipreading, he can warn us of likely pitfalls. He also provides a wide variety of practice material that we can speak to our mirrors or that others can speak to us, helping us to gain familiarity and confidence in seeing speech.

John Chaloner Woods was a professional photographer and also a 'graduate' of the lipreading classes held by the ILEA and the City Lit.

'Since I broke my glasses, I've not been able to hear so well.'

Lipreading

A GUIDE FOR BEGINNERS

John Chaloner Woods

JOHN MURRAY

© The Estate of John Chaloner Woods 1986

First published 1986
by John Murray (Publishers) Ltd
50 Albemarle Street, London w1x 4bd

Typeset by Inforum Ltd, Portsmouth
Printed and bound in Great Britain
by Richard Clay (The Chaucer Press), Bungay, Suffolk

British Library CIP Data
Woods, John Chaloner
  Lipreading : a guide for beginners.
  1. Lipreading
  I. Title
  362.4′2   HV2487
  isbn 0–7195–4341–X

Contents

Introduction

For myself, as for many others, hearing loss has come as I have grown older. At the approach of seventy, many of us have difficulty with the high-pitched sounds. We may retain hearing for the vowels which have more energy than the high frequencies. These have little energy and are lost with age. Apparently, bats flying in the dark make a sound of such high frequency that only dogs and children up to the age of seven are capable of hearing it. The bats use it as a sort of radar to locate the position of objects ahead. Adults are most unlikely to hear it, showing that an unimportant degree of hearing loss occurs early in life. The ear drum consists of a small piece of skin capable of vibrating in accordance with the frequencies of the sound reaching it. Presumably the more perfect the elasticity of the drum, the greater the volume of sounds receivable.

For a very long time we can go to the theatre, to meetings, have discussions, listen to radio and television and still hear everything perfectly well. Then gradually people who will not speak up, or mumble, seem to have increased since we were young. They do seem not to teach children in schools to speak properly. Even many politicians and public speakers seem never to have learned elocution. Members of the public, interviewed on television or radio often speak so badly that it is a waste of time to listen. We all know that to hear we must listen, but it all gets very frustrating. This is what happened to me.

Eventually, I acquired quite a skill at placing my hand precisely in a kind of cup shape at an exact distance, to my ear, thereby improving the power to listen. Of course, other people noticed what I was doing and dropped hints that my ears might need a visit to the doctor for syringing, when I could hear perfectly well in the ordinary way. At last I gave in and went to a specialist recommended for treating wax in the ears, near Harley Street. He used what he called his 'Hoover' instead of syringing. After the second visit, I went, cheque book in hand, to his secretary and asked, 'How much?' What she replied sounded alarmingly like

'Fifty'. So I put my hand to my ear with a querulous expression and she said 'Fifteen pounds'.

You can guess the next thing: I went to my National Health doctor, and he gave me a letter to the Consultant at the hospital. He had an audiometric test done and prescribed a hearing aid, which I received some time after – all free.

A photographer by trade, I had a little pendulum in my darkroom. It made a 'tick' every second by which I used to time the exposure when making prints. For quite some time previously it was becoming difficult to hear. I found I could see a shadow cast by the pendulum from the safe-light and I carried on until I realised it had lost its 'tick' altogether. I examined it and could find no explanation. There was not really anything to go wrong. The day I got my hearing aid, I went into my darkroom and just gave the pendulum a push. It 'ticked' loud and clear!

In the case of deafness due to age the hearing loss is in the high frequency range of sounds more than in the lower frequencies. The hearing aid attempts to increase the volume of the high frequencies more than the volume of the lower ones; this succeeds in producing a distortion to balance the distortion created by the hearing loss. In good conditions this works pretty well, and makes words lost without the aid audible with it. However, there are a great many occasions when the hearing aid is unable to help on its own and that is when Lipreading has its very important role to play.

Everyone born with normal sight and hearing begins, soon after birth, to attach meaning to, for example, a friendly face, or an angry word. Babies learn by direct aural and visual observance and imitation of what is seen and heard. The signals sent by the nerves of the ears and eyes are translated by the brain into sounds and sight. The brain develops and adds to its store of information with the growth of the child into a person. But during a working life, some instinctive learning skills are forgotten.

I have a strong memory of what I felt at my first Lipreading class where voiceless speech was used. Since then I have observed how newcomers respond when they join. This leaves me with little doubt that a long-unused skill is aroused, as meaning is found from this strange experience. When hearing was unimpaired there was no need to notice what speech looked like – it was audible and required no conscious attention to its appearance. At the first session when speech is deliberately silent the neglected skill begins to return: we see words, a phrase, or perhaps a simple sentence. We see the sound of speech. Practice in this new use of our eyes gradually builds a visual vocabulary.

Progress will be more rapid if you can go to a class, but self-help alone with diligent use of a mirror, or with a friend or friends, or with the television, and practice in voiceless speech, can cause great strides to be made in successfully seeing speech. The word most commonly used in this country for the skill needed to learn to see speech is 'Lipreading' and classes will generally be called lipreading classes. Sadly many older people with a common form of hearing loss, may be put off the idea because it sounds like learning another language. Actually it is learning to see a language already known and comes naturally by practice, leading out of unused memory from past experience.

Tests have been made, choosing two groups of people, one group consisting of those with normal hearing and no experience of lipreading, the other of people with hearing loss and practice in lipreading. Single words, without voice, were spoken to each member of each group. The surprising result was the degree of success scored by the group with no experience of lipreading. This demonstrates the probability that hearing people all have some residual sense of the visibility of speech.

The adventure of learning to see speech, is not at all like entering a dark tunnel. Signposts are soon found, to encourage further exploration. The photographs reproduced here are ones which I took after much study and discussion with my teacher. They are signposts pointing to the visibility of certain speech sounds. They represent those sounds which can be shown as static shapes, but it must be remembered that they are always seen in movement during speech. The deliberate and accurate formation of these shapes during speech helps visibility and therefore understanding. They often provide the key to a whole word or sentence.

Practice in speaking without voice is important not only to those wishing to communicate with the deaf but also to the deaf themselves when learning to see voiceless speech. Both should *feel* that the voiceless speech is well formed. Respect for these signposts will help conversation, preventing exaggerated mouthing, or careless pronunciation.

1 Seeing the Sound of Speech

Lipreading classes

When I went to the hearing aid centre and was having an impression of my ear made, I asked the lady doing it about lipreading. On hearing the word, she suddenly became enthusiastic and said, 'I'll get you details. We have a class at the hospital. I'll find the day and time of the next class.' I had only a vague idea of what lipreading was. In the back of my mind was the thought that my hearing loss, although mild, might be progressive and that my hearing aid might need supplementing.

So I turned up at the appropriate time, wondering if I would be accepted and what a lipreading class would be like – a bit like my first day at school. I was welcomed and given a most interesting introduction to the subject by practising lipreading speech without voice. I met people who regarded any degree of hearing loss as a simple matter of fact, rather like a game of cards. Some get a good hand, some a bad one, but whatever you have been dealt, that is the hand you must play and you might as well enjoy the game.

With a comparatively mild loss, you feel a bit of a fraud because you can hear many things perfectly well. You should not worry on that account. It is a good thing to meet people who speak quite naturally about their own deafness. One said to me, 'Mine started while I was still at primary school.' I realised that was why he was difficult to hear because he could not hear his own voice very well. Another could speak normally, but was profoundly deaf. His hearing had been destroyed by disease at a later age, so he knew what speech sounded like and had learned to control his own voice, although he could not hear it. He carried on a conversation with the teacher lipreading what she said and speaking what he had to say.

The pity of it is that there are comparatively few classes throughout the country. I regard myself as extremely lucky for two reasons. Firstly because I went straight to a class from the

9

hearing aid centre. Secondly because I never thought that I was, at my age, embarking upon the acquisition of a new skill. If I had stopped to think, I might never have started. Now I have no regrets and I can face the years ahead with a moderate skill. There are innumerable occasions when, with a combination of a hearing aid, lipreading and my residual hearing, I can get the message – in shops, at meetings, in conversations, and of course with the television. In conditions with excessive background noise, such as a crowded room with everyone talking (or shouting), the hearing aid 'aids' *all* the noise, not what you want to hear. Only lipreading and experience can overcome these conditions.

The responsibility for the care of adults with hearing loss has been allotted to the Local Authorities' Adult Education Departments, which are also responsible for a large number of different subjects from domestic upholstery to various sports activities. Persistent efforts by various – mainly voluntary – organisations have gradually caused Councils to become enlightened about the special requirements of those with hearing difficulties. Progress in this direction is regularly impeded by lack of funding. Enquiry should be made to the local Adult Education Officer to find what provision is made for those with hearing loss, whether lipreading classes are held in your area or whether there are any plans for the future. If not, why not? Ask in a nice sort of way, remembering he may have troubles of his own, like his job!

It astonishes me that although 1.6 million hearing aids have been issued nationwide, lack of demand for lipreading classes is given as the reason that there are so pitifully few. My experience tells me that the hearing aid solves many problems, but leaves many unsolved. It may well be that, with the older population, classes on a rehabilitative theme offering perhaps six introductory sessions in the first place, would be more suitable for those recently involved in hearing difficulty. These could be on: how the hearing aid works, or doesn't, what to do about it, when and when not to wear it, what it can realistically be expected to do. Then a lesson on sound, its quirks, what happens to it when passed through another device, like the aid or telephone; followed by one on our alphabet: sounds made by letters are different from the names of the letters. Then something about the language, its richness and peculiarities. Then how hearing people communicate and what hearing loss implies and what changes in the situation there might be. If you agree that such a six-week course on the lines suggested would interest you enough to go to it, write to or get in touch with the organisations listed on p. 000.

There may be variations throughout the country about charging a fee for classes, but for pensioners and the disabled, it is likely to be moderate or nominal. Complications can arise if the class you choose is organised by an authority other than the one in whose area you live. If you have doubts about committing yourself to one period a week during school term time, you should see the teacher, and also enquire whether other subjects relating to listening and hearing are dealt with.

Members of a class, of course, come from all sorts of occupations. Very often, introductions are made using Christian names: the qualification for membership is hearing loss, a disability which creates mutual respect. A pleasant atmosphere in the class comes from the keenness and concentration of everyone, teacher and students. After about an hour it is usual to have a coffee break. At that point everyone very often starts talking, all at once. If you have discovered that you cannot get on with your hearing aid in a room full of people, now is your chance to find out how to cope.

A doctor psychologist once told me, 'Weigh up the pros and cons and give the most careful thought to matters which are not really important, but with the really important ones, act upon a hunch.' I am convinced that anyone who has worked alone, or with a friend or friends upon the exercises suggested in this book, is now up against a decision upon a really important matter. So do not think for too long about a lipreading class. If you can find one, join it! There is no school attendance officer to catch you if you play truant. I have noticed on occasion when there is something of wide appeal on the TV that numbers in class drop. There was once – I think it was the last class in the term – when I and the teacher were the class. So I had a session of private tuition which I think interested both of us, and encouraged me.

Hearing aids

The danger of relying entirely upon the hearing aid is that you might slide back into the state of isolation which drove you to the hearing aid centre in the first place. The hearing aid can be a trap, insofar as it does not solve all the hearing problems. It is a truism

11

to say that to hear we must listen. Once deafness comes on us, we must listen with our eyes as well as ears. It takes a positive effort. Not listening is a negative and a dangerous habit. If you can read a book or a paper all evening while the radio or television is on in the same room, you are acquiring a skill which is the opposite of what you want for hearing. Be careful. If you are tired, it would be better to have 'forty winks' in your chair or go to bed.

The best way to look at it is that both the hearing aid and lipreading are adjuncts to listening, not a substitute for hearing, at least for those who have any useful hearing left. (For more on hearing aids see p. 59.)

Approaches to Lipreading

There are two mental approaches to lipreading – the analytic and the synthetic or rhythmic. The analytic seeks primarily to read each sound accurately and translate the whole into the language correctly. The synthetic seeks to observe the flow or rhythm of the language, getting the meaning or sense of the message with the help of intuition, foresight and hindsight, and not interrupting the flow by too much analytical precision. There is a good case for both methods: the analytic in the early stages and a combination of both methods when the skills have advanced enough. Nobody knows exactly what goes on in the brain when we learn to 'see' sounds by lipreading, nor does a teacher know how students learn. Probably those whose approach is more analytic will find the synthetic method too vague and the synthetic learners will tend to find analytic drill too boring, so a bit of each is used. I have been persuaded not to use the word 'invisible' in relation to the sounds most diffucult to see, because there may always be someone who can see some little movement of a muscle somewhere. Sheer mental agility, in spite of there being no obvious context or clue, may provide the solution.

A lively memory is a great help in lipreading, and should be developed. In these matters some of us whose hearing loss is due to age may feel that youth has the advantage of us! As the 'oldest inhabitant' in my class, I do sometimes wonder to what extent you can teach an old dog new tricks. In my younger days I heard the expression 'second childhood' applied to other people and I thought I understood it. Now, particularly when I have just made a stupid mistake, I begin to wonder. Childhood is a time when the capacity to learn is at its highest.

Anticipation and context

Lipreading practice with qualified teachers is usually without voice because this concentrates the attention on seeing. Anticipation, mental alertness and alacrity are encouraged to help the lipreader. It is much easier to lipread words you are expecting. I remember in a very early class when I was thinking ahead and was sure a certain word was bound to come, but – you know the way it is – I forgot the word, my mind went blank. Sure enough the word came and I lipread it! It was the strangest feeling. The word lost in my mind reappeared by lipreading.

The most difficult exercise in lipreading is when there is no context. When there is some clue as to the subject, the difficulty is reduced. For instance, at the breakfast table, if someone asks you, 'Please pass the marmalade,' this is very much easier to lipread than some comment about the foreign news, especially if you haven't seen the paper yet. Therefore, if you want a person to lipread what you have to say, start by providing a context or clue, if one does not already exist. In a lot of everyday situations we all get the message, whether we hear the words or not, if we see the speaker's face and gesture. 'How are you?' 'What a beautiful day.' 'Can't stop now, must catch this bus.' Or (yawn) 'I'm off to bed now.' There is little difficulty in getting the message, with or without hearing or lipreading. The context of the occasion helps the lipreader to anticipate what may be coming. 'I saw a conjurer saw a girl in half.' The context makes it easy to recognise the same sound (saw) as being two distinct words with different meanings, as we already do, reading it in print or hearing it.

Lipreading is concerned with sounds, not spelling. As a baby and toddler you learnt the sound, meaning and appearance of speech, before learning the alphabet. Now, you must think only of sound, meaning, and what it looks like on the face, but not spelt out on the page. The context sorts out words making the same sound. Bow may mean the bough of a tree, the bow of a boat or a bending of the body. The context sorts them out. The problem is not new to lipreading. What is new to lipreading, is the context having to sort out words which may sound different but look the same because they make the same lip movement. For instance the words 'pop' and 'bomb'. There are many more.

How long does it take to learn?

A number of factors are involved – age, memory, aptitude, degree of hearing loss, the urgency of the desire to learn. The milder the degree of hearing loss, the longer it may take to learn because a hearing aid is enough help in many situations. The greater the degree of hearing loss, the more urgent it becomes to remember to practise whenever possible on most daily occasions.

The goal for most of us will be to combine hearing and lipreading together, but it is necessary to acquire enough skill at lipreading without voice. If you want an idea how long it takes to become a really expert lipreader, I know of someone struck by total deafness through an illness. It was just as he had qualified for a good career, but the deafness meant he had to abandon it. As a result of necessity, sheer character and courage, working hard with six lessons a week with various teachers for five years, an expert lipreader was created, able to work in another branch of the same profession in which he had originally qualified.

Using the photographs

The photographs can be used on your own, or in conjunction with a mirror. They help you judge the effect on your own face, getting the feel of each lip shape, practising with whole words and short phrases as well, seeing movement from shape to shape. Undoubtedly, this could teach one to lipspeak better, and would serve as an introduction to lipreading.

I can imagine a husband attending a lipreading class and his wife studying the photographs reproduced here with a mirror, and so finding communication between themselves much easier. It has been said that a husband cannot teach his wife to drive a car, and so it may be that a wife cannot teach her husband to lipread. Only the couple can decide about that for themselves. The fact to be faced is that you can introduce yourself to lipreading with a mirror. You can check the appearance of words or phrases which occur in lipreading and, of course, in lipspeaking.

Learning outside a class

Failing a class within practicable distance, it would be ideal to find someone, or a small group, who are willing to attend regular sessions for practice of lipreading and lipspeaking. Probably an hour is a long enough session for the intense concentration required for lipreading without voice, or even half an hour. Qualified teachers of lipreading go to a great deal of trouble to make what is to be lipread interesting and relevant to the lip-shapes being studied. It would be wise, if two, or more, friends arrange to have practice sessions together, to decide at the beginning who is to be lipspeaker and who lipreader. This could mean taking turns, but it does also make clear who, as the lipspeaker, must prepare the subject for each occasion. This in itself becomes part of the learning process, because it involves consideration of what is easy to lipread and what is difficult or nearly impossible.

Phrases with the same rhythm

When the one who is to be lipspeaker (for practice sessions, that means without voice) is preparing for a session, homophonous words like bough and bow (which sound and look the same) are not so much a problem, because the context distinguishes them. The real problem comes with phrases which have the same rhythm.

It distresses me when my daughters argue.

It distresses me when my corsets are new.

Try those words on the lips of your image in the mirror. (The really expert lipreader might spot the difference between 'daughters' and 'corsets' and 'argue' and 'are new'.) Then try the whole sentences. Have a look at the photographs. Each of them is a basic lip shape you need to make properly to produce the particular sound which occurs in speech. The 'au' and 'or' sounds in 'daughters' and 'corsets' is the long vowel 'aw' (p. 25). The 'ar' in 'argue' is the same as in 'are' – the long vowel 'ah' (p. 25). The 'ue' in 'argue' is the same as in 'new' – the double vowel – 'ewe' or 'u'.

The rhythm of the two phrases is very much the same, and the lipreader might well be pleased if either phrase had been read correctly. If not, the result could be some hilarious laughter, a welcome relief from the concentration needed for lipreading. Context would make one or other of the phrases nonsense, and so simplify things.

Party tricks

If there are any occasions when it would be wise to hide hearing difficulty, they are few indeed. It will be found that admitting hearing difficulty generally produces a very favourable response with most hearing people. So don't try to hide the hearing aid. People often notice it and speak a little louder and more clearly and kindly.

As far as possible take a positive attitude to your hearing loss and avoid 'opting out', lest it becomes a habit. Even cocktail parties with lots of people all talking at the top of their voices should be experienced. It is possible to invent a technique for having a conversation with a friend in such conditions. You have to get very close, with your hearing aid well positioned (or even switched off) so that you can see your friend speaking. It is well worth experimenting. But you may be forgiven if you find you 'opt out' by being engaged for the next party.

I will let you into a secret I have discovered. The really expert lipreaders have found a way to cope with such situations. Lipreading is always rather hard work and can be avoided by keeping talking yourself as long as you can hold a person's interest, then slide away with the friendliest of smiles.

Tips for family and friends

Family and friends are a problem when you start lipreading. Not everyone takes kindly to hints that exaggerated mouthing of words may be more difficult to lipread than careful speech, pronouncing every syllable, and that anything like a shout is more difficult, too. It is like those people who think it helps to shout down the phone when calling America or that they make themselves understood by shouting slowly in English at French waiters.

Hand in front of mouth.

Constant movement of the head.

Smiling while you talk.

Looking the other way.

These are among the things to encourage your friends to avoid.

Long ago, before I had any reason to think about hearing, I devised a way to speak to my father after he suffered hearing loss. I would say the first few words in an ordinary voice. When he showed any sign of attention, I would repeat the words in much the same voice and he would generally hear. My mother used to say, 'He can hear what he wants to.' I know now that after I had got his attention, he then heard me speak, saw my face and probably used a primitive form of lipreading.

A good way to train family and friends who need to communicate vocally is to get a discussion going on the lip shapes illustrated here: as to whether they are exaggerated or not. Keep the discussion going as long as they will play. It may develop into an argument, because colloquial speech is often too rapid for the shapes to be formed properly. Anyway, to draw out the opinions of lipspeakers, lipreaders and those who just talk, is a tactful way of avoiding too many 'do's and don'ts', which are liable to be resented. One thing that this should teach is that a lipreader takes longer to interpret the shapes seen, than a hearing person takes to recognise the sounds, at least until the lipreader becomes more expert than I and many others have become.

In recent years there has been much written about the unspoken 'body language' that we all use, consciously and unconsciously, to supplement what we are saying – facial expressions, gestures, positions of arms and legs. Lipreading is, if you like, the most sophisticated body language of all. Research has proved that hearing people lipread individual test words (without voice) as well as deaf people. This indicates that we all lipread to some extent. In these days, town dwellers in particular need to watch a companion in the tube or a crowded restaurant. It is a question of building on this.

Our eyes have to build a skill upon not-too-well-observed, fleeting shapes upon the face of a speaker. It is a marvel really that the brain is capable of doing it. When I mentioned lipreading to a friend, who I could see had difficulty with hearing, he said, 'I have not got the type of brain which would adapt to such a process.' A better attitude to the problem would be that of the man who, when asked if he could play the violin, answered, 'I don't know, I've never tried.' So if you don't know whether you can lipread, this book should give you a chance to try.

I have often thought to myself that I have learned a certain word after failing to recognise it many times, when at last I have spotted it successfully. There may always be, after a little time, another failure with the same word. I am writing of lipreading without voice. If one can ignore failures and remember successes, the balance gradually moves towards success. Remembering the difficulty, success is its own reward, well-earned and highly valued on any occasion, even if it is only one sentence that one has captured.

2   Starting with the Mirror

If you have bought this book, haven't been to a lipreading class, have no one at the moment with whom you can practice lip shapes, or feel shy about it, then this is when the mirror comes in. Say 'peacock' with and without voice, watching your image in the mirror. When you say 'pea' the lips part, showing a wide opening for the 'ee' sound. The 'c' and 'ck' of cock are not usually visible but the syllable 'cock' appears as a slight movement of the jaw. Incidentally, 'peacock' is a good example of a word where seeing and hearing dovetail in for the benefit of lipreaders with some hearing. The 'pea' is easy to see while the 'cock' is difficult to see but easy to hear. There are plenty of others.

It is quite a job to arrange to work with a mirror. So to save all the trouble of setting it up in a good light and a quiet private place, it will be worthwhile arranging somewhere easy to work in at any time. It may also be worth buying a transparent perspex cookery book holder from W H Smith to put this book in. Don't work too hard with the mirror but have a rest and a change by watching television or having a chat with someone. Then try to remember to watch for lip shapes when there is a reasonable close-up of someone talking on television. Not to worry if you become interested and forget to watch.

Using a mirror is quite hard work. Remember that this is a less than ideal way to introduce lipreading and lipspeaking. See if you can start to get into a habit of watching people's faces when they speak, rather than just their lips. Experiment with switching off your hearing aid, or taking it off, or not putting it on. (Warning:

without the hearing aid, there is a risk outdoors when there is traffic.) Lipreading and lipspeaking is a live method of communication by live people. Reading about it, is an intellectual exercise, which could become rather deadly. So if you feel a bit bored with it all as you read, let your mind wander in a search for somebody who might share a live interest, as a substitute for a teacher and a class. If you could get a real person, instead of your own image in the mirror, to speak the things I suggest, you would be getting real practice. But do not stop using the mirror then. Let your friends use it, too.

3 P B M

So let us start with the lip shape P.B.M. (see photograph). This shape appears the same for each sound. It is also one of the easiest to recognise. The words 'pea,' 'bee,' 'me' spoken voicelessly, separately, alone and without any clue or context, are visually indistinguishable. Given a context, this is no problem.

> A bunch of sweet peas.

> A swarm of bees.

> Who? Me?

Incidentally, did you notice that a 'bunch of sweet peas' has the PBM shape twice? And then you say, 'Who? Me?' your expression changes? This is all part of lipreading and lipspeaking. Lipreading requires concentration – you cannot take your eyes off the lipspeaker's face even for a moment – and observation trained by practice and more practice. Lipspeaking requires study of the techniques of speech and empathy with the reader.

I have chosen the P B M to show what you are in for. Over and over again, I have failed to read a voiceless sentence in class because I thought a word included the sound M when it was in fact a P or B. With the M sound I could not make sense, but my brain obstinately refused to remember to try P or B which would have given me the word. What a joy it is now in normal life to hear and lipread together and never be caught by the P B M shape. It is

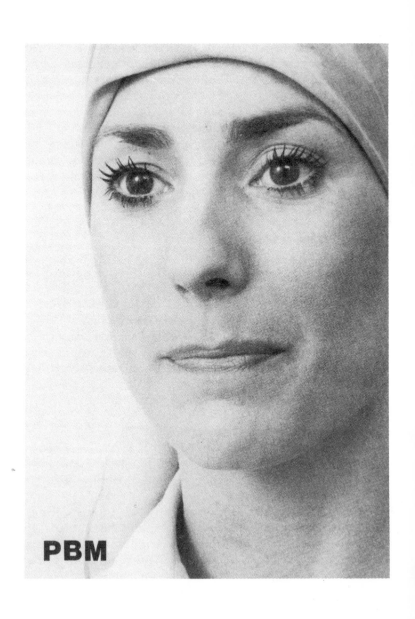

easily seen-and-heard. The reason for this is that, for those with hearing, M is a nasal sound, and as such is easily distinguished by ear. B is distinguished from P because of its voiced quality. Listening practice will show those with some hearing that many lipreading problems will fade when they are watching and listening.

I think that with voiceless lipreading, it is sometimes just possible to detect M as very slightly different from the other two, but it is difficult to be sure that there has not been a context clue.

Here are suggestions for mirror practice:

> Being a Member of Parliament makes him an MP.

> Perhaps he'll become Prime Minister.

Note how you say MP and Prime Minister, and some other words like 'empire' and 'import'. The M and P come together – the visual result is the closing of the lips once, not twice.

> His performance prevented a bitter battle being
> fought between the opposition and the government.

> Preparation for black immigrants means involvement
> in better provision for their accommodation.

> Better employment becomes a primary purpose.

> Many believe it all began with a great big bang.

Another suggestion for practice, is to watch a speaker on TV and count the number of times you see the PBM form on the speaker's face. You may notice F looking rather like PBM. Say F, B. M:

> funny mummy, funny bunny.

Then to keep up interest – count the F shapes only, or SH, TH, or L shapes only. Such exercises are basic eye training which, when combined with some voiceless training, will later enable you to get the most out of your combination of lipreading and hearing aid.

In a class a qualified teacher might spend three sessions on the PBM lip shape, taking each one at a time. Of necessity, many other lip shapes will come into sentences, and gradually familiarity with others will be introduced. The limitations of the printed word mean that you are thrown on to your own devices to get some practice with the mirror. Invent little phrases to lipspeak to your image.

A penny for your thoughts.

You can observe the P and three long vowel sounds – AW (the same sound), the second starting with Y, which is not very seeable, the third with TH. Say, 'For your thoughts'. Perhaps you can see the Y, perhaps not. You can exaggerate the Y a little to make it more visible.

Perhaps we should buy a mini.

Just observe what you can (or cannot – like the H) see – two P's, an S, a W, EE again, SH (a good one to see), a B and an M.

Peter Piper picked a peck of pickled pepper.

Many a slip 'twixt cup and lip.

There is an L twice, a W again, an X to compare with an S.

Sing a song of sixpence.

A CE to compare with S. That is why only the sound matters in lipreading – not the spelling. Consider these:

Bough	Bow
Cough	Cof
Fight	Fite
Height	Hite
Laugh	Lahf
Rough	Ruf
Thorough	Thuhra
Though	Tho
Thought	Thawt
Through	Throo

Be thankful you are learning to lipread and are not a foreigner trying to learn English or a child learning to spell!

4   F, V, PH

Visually, these sounds are identical in appearance and easy to see, but the V has a different audible sound, and that difference can be important. The correct lip shape is the lower lip coming up to the upper front teeth.

Few looked at the view.

Sight alone cannot distinguish between the first and last words 'few' and 'view', but there is an audible difference which should be detectable with a hearing aid.

Very few photographed the view.

When watching speech without voice, words beginning with V often cause difficulty because the F or PH is more common, and V is unexpected. The solution, with experience, is to try the effect of substituting a V for an F and getting the sense.

'Full of flowers' is an example of one word ending with F and the next word beginning with F. Normal speech produces one slightly prolonged F. 'Fifty-five' is a number you should read accurately, but 'fifteen' or 'fifty' are numbers easily misread. All '–teens' and '–tys' are danger signals for lipreading. We are taught always to check when these occur. The way to do this is to ask the question, 'Did you say fifteen?' and the answer will be 'Yes' or 'No', so telling you which it was. You must not ask, 'Did you say fifty or fifteen?' because the answer you will get will leave you in as much doubt as you were in before. 'Yes' or 'No' should be quite clear, at least if you can see the speaker's face.

Mental alacrity is needed again to avoid selecting the wrong lipshape out of the three, F, V or PH – finish, television and telephone. Say this to the mirror.

Father fought for his fee for providing further food.

It is a rather silly sentence, but it contains several F's and also the set of long vowels which occur in lipreading (see p. 25). Notice that the words 'fought', 'for' and 'four' have the same vowel

23

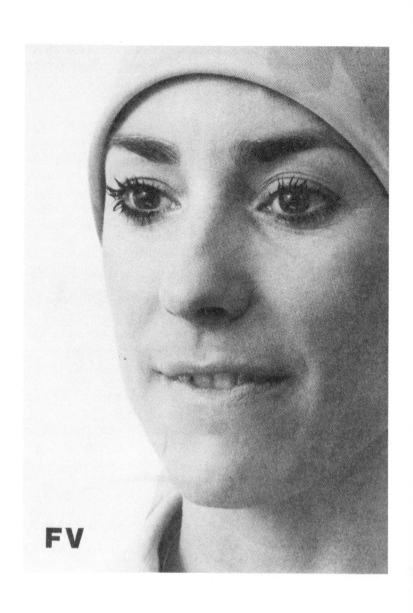

FV

shape and sound regardless of spelling. Practice in the mirror with these words:

fun	pun
bun	mum
muff	tough
trough	fool
pool	mule

and watch the difference between the F shape and the PBM shape. Also notice that GH joins FVPH in looks and sound on these occasions.

5   The Long Vowels – AH AW (OR) OO EE ER (UR) – and the Importance of Stress

A, E, I, O, U, the vowels of the alphabet that you learnt in school, have little to do with the vowels seen and heard in speech. So let's concentrate on what we can see. You must work with the signpost photographs in front of you, and the mirror.

Say AH: the vowel in car, heart, laugh, part, rasp, tart, half. Watching your face in the mirror, you will see that the AH sound is made by dropping the jaw to open the mouth (voiceless) – just what a baby does as a spoonful of food approaches.

Say AW: the same movement as AH except the corners of the mouth move inwards and lips forward as the mouth opens, and the jaw may jut forward a bit. Awful, bought, caught, fort, George, jaw, law, lord, more, roar, tort, taught, wart, (your, as sometimes pronounced).

Say OO: the jaw comes up and makes the OO sound. Who, coup, fool, ghoul, loot, two, rue, rule, school, truce. Words like 'new', 'few' are subtly different – they are double vowels (see p. 47). They look similar, but not quite the same to the sharp eye.

EE is a clear vowel to see, if properly spoken. The corners of the mouth are widened, almost a smile. It is a wide, narrow, horizontal shape. A lot depends upon the face of the speaker, whether

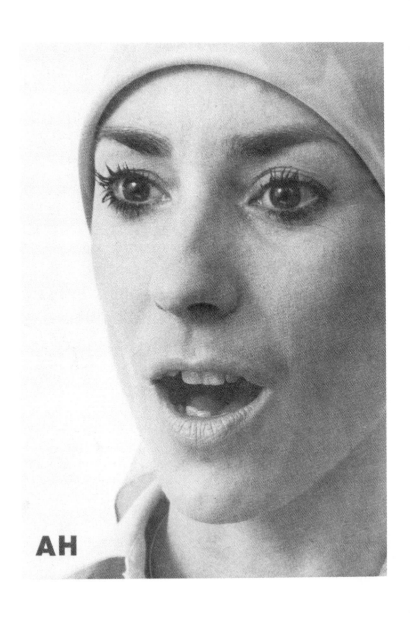

AH

AW

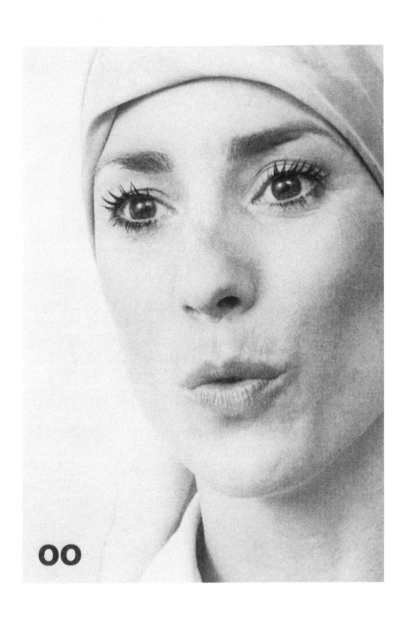

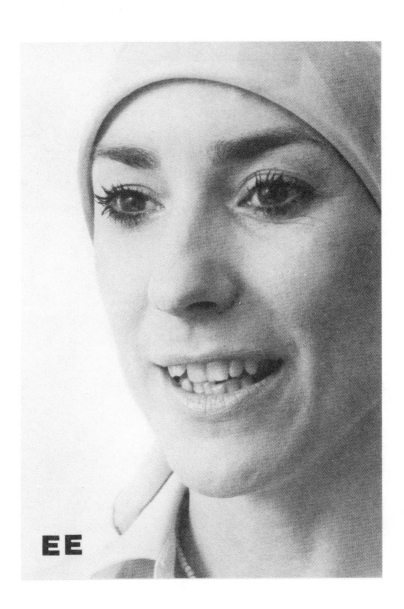

EE

29

UR

the movement shows teeth naturally or not. It is possible to make the EE sound more visible, but don't overdo it. Practise in the mirror – watch other people. Say to the mirror 'it's easy' – the I is a short vowel (see p.50) and the EA is the long vowel EE. There is not much difference to see, but plenty to hear.

Finally there is a long vowel UR or ER. Say 'bird', 'curd', 'dirty', 'flirt', 'hurt', 'jerk', 'learn', 'mirth', 'purpose', 'sir', 'turf', 'verb', 'word', 'earn', 'urn'. The corners of the mouth come inwards, the jaw drops slightly and the lower lip moves forward.

The aim of practice is to work towards instant recognition by sight of these long vowels as confirmation of what you hear. (I can hear when I can see.) I have found it a great encouragement when the television news reader disappears, and is replaced by a map, but goes on talking. I lose what she is saying until she returns to the screen again, but then I can see and hear once more. The time spent on these long vowels will not be wasted. Teachers using voiceless speech may use a whole session on each of the long vowels. Study the changes on your own image's face, as you go from one long vowel to another. Think of someone you have observed on the telly who speaks practically without opening his lips, like a ventriloquist. Now try to say the long vowels AH, AW, OO, EE, ER, keeping your lips nearly closed. Remember to open your mouth when lipspeaking, even if you have not the perfect set of teeth. Few have. Anyhow, all the lipreaders will forgive your imperfections (if any) if you make the shapes clearly.

Some practice sentences for the mirror, or better still a friend who will read them, voiceless, to you:

Aren't her school fees awful?

Articled clerks are taught by lawyers.

He's a keen cheese eater.

He keeps geese to feed on the lawn.

The early bird earns the worm.

His car ought to do thirty-five mpg.

Too much heat soon burns up food.

Forty furtive fools feeding fast.

You ought not to do that.

31

Stress

Say the last sentence in the list above as you would to a child, quite quickly and then very carefully, as in the photographs. Think also of the rhythm of the sentence, with the accent on 'ought' and then on 'do', or possibly, the accent on 'not', and then on 'do'. This is all part of lipspeaking and lipreading.

Stress is especially important in English, since it changes the meaning. It is possible to take English sentences, *e.g.* 'Would you like soup today?' and stress a different word five times, with five different meanings. It is possible to teach a good lipreader or lipspeaker to look for this stress. More energy is put into the stressed syllable, and the vowel or consonant is elongated. Look at the difference between, 'She's always shopping in *Oxford* Street.' (Not Bond Street, not Tottenham Court Road.) 'She's *always* shopping in Oxford Street.' (Not just once a month or annually.)

6 SH

Let's have a nice one to see next: SH. It is very visible and audible and often appears in speech. It is the sound you make when you put your finger in front of your mouth to mean 'hush'. Unfortunately, it is very much like some others – the soft CH (chicken, urchin, machine), J (jeep), and G (George). These are the main alternatives, but you get SH sounds in ocean, tension, session, caution, sure. We sometimes notice in class that when speaking without voice, it is difficult to say SH without making any sound; and the SH sound is one that a hearing aid may be boosting for those with a hearing loss in the high frequency sounds.

Surely merchant ships should be cautious on the ocean. Their engines and machinery are subject to tensions.

The urchin look makes a smashing fashion for teenagers.

George took the picture.

TU is a borderline SH shape: mature, overture. Some people

SH

make it a T shape, some a TCH. I think it *looks* like SH, even when pronounced T. Actually the sound in 'picture', 'mature' is CH which is a combination of T plus SH. This is why it resembles SH because the initial T is drowned by the bigger SH.

Of course, in spite of the spelling, 'Christians' are not admitted into this chapter, nor 'chorus girls'. They go with the gutteral K. Like the hard C it is a sound made in the throat – very difficult to see, but easy to hear. 'Ginger', 'jackals' and 'Germans' are welcome, so are 'chickens' and 'cherries'.

Sunshine and showers is sometimes the weather forecast. Repeated rapidly it can become a tongue twister. Suggest to someone that they say sunshine and showers as fast as they can and count how many times before it becomes 'shunsine and sowers'. Ask a friend to say 'surely slogans on shirts are out of fashion now'. You can get friends unwittingly to co-operate in your studies. If they spot your game, they may be glad to help, you never know!

See what happens when one shape ends a word and begins the next: 'George generally . . .' 'Cash shows . . .' Words are what we have to see, and hear, so the more we know about them, and what people do to them as they speak, the better.

7 TH and the Invisibles: T, D, hard G, hard C, hard K

Another consonant sound to follow SH. First study the photograph, and how the sound is made. Get the feel of it, and note what you see in the mirror. People vary quite a lot. The shape is just the tip of the tongue peeping through between the teeth. Say to your mirror, 'I think this thing thoroughly disproves the theory'. It is easy to see TH when people part their lips as they speak, and sometimes it is visible from a side view of the speaker. The sound is not very easy to hear, but is a valuable signpost when seen. After the complications of the SH, J, etc., sounds, TH has the great advantage that if TH is what you saw, then TH it is. Say 'the fifth thing' and see what happens. With most people the two TH's will be seen as one, but just a tiny bit longer. Some-

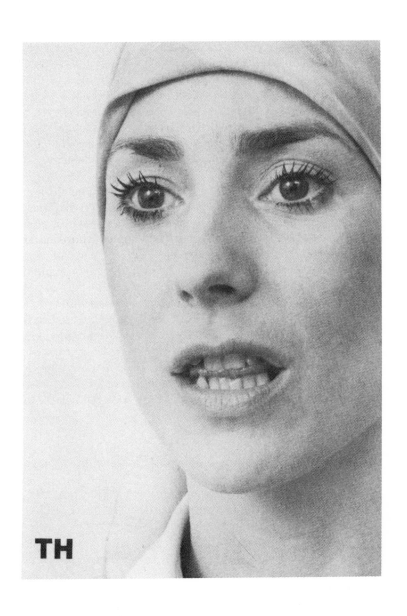

TH

times, a person trying to be helpful, may put the tongue right out, with the misguided idea that 'mouthing' words helps defective hearing.

The TH sound can only be made with the breath passing through the teeth with the tongue in the position illustrated. It is not a loud sound and missing teeth, or dentures, may affect it adversely. Lips not properly parted conceal the sight of the sound, and you may still need the help of mental alacrity, and guesswork as well.

Following the study of the TH sound, now is a good time to consider the sounds T, D, and N which are made by the tongue just behind the top front teeth. Many who have had lessons in public speaking have been taught to make these sounds effectively. The words 'art' and 'and' are distinguished by making the T more explosive than the D. They are both made by forcing the breath between the tongue and the top front teeth, the 'd' being made audible less forcefully with voice. Compare the words 'candid' and 'tempted', and feel the difference. Spoken well the Ts and Ds should be definitely audible, but are unlikely to be visible, so it is not possible to illustrate them with photographs.

N is also made with the tongue pressed up at the back of the top front teeth, but the breath is prevented from passing so it goes out through the nose, with a nasal sound. (When the nasal passage is blocked by a common cold the 'd' sound results. The word 'nine' sounds like 'dide'.)

T and D are invisible to all intents and purposes for most of us. They give exercise to our guessing abilities. 'Tedious' is such a word. Speak it to your image in the mirror and see. Hard C and hard G and K are other examples of invisibles. Try 'cock', 'dog', 'cat', 'good', 'god' and 'tack'. Compare 'dog' and 'cat' and 'good' and see what difference there is.

I have often been puzzled by the word 'car'. It looks like 'ah'. Gradually I am learning that 'ah' is 'car'. I have also been stumped by 'dog' and 'doctor' more often than not. I shall never forget someone who came to the class occasionally. He was profoundly deaf. The teacher gave us each (without voice) one word to lipread. When she came to him she said 'Dog'. He paused for a moment, then said, 'Well, it looks like a dog.' So when I call them invisibles, maybe they are not so to the expert.

The one saving grace of the (to most of us) 'invisibles' is that they tend to be quite audible, so that when it is possible to use both hearing and lipreading together, one should get the message.

The words 'eight', 'nine' and 'ten' are difficult to distinguish by sight alone. Check by asking, 'Did you say nine?' If the answer is 'No', you must then ask again, 'Did you say eight?' If the answer is 'no' you will know the number must have been 'ten'.

Logical anticipation in the context, facial expression, small gestures, all help the eyes to see the speech. Emphasis on a phrase, a word, or just a syllable all play their part in making the meaning seeable, provided nothing is allowed to distract the eyes from watching the face of the speaker.

Whether or not you are in the habit of watching the news-readers on TV, do keep reminding yourself to look out for the signposts of visible speech introduced so far – there are more to come. The human mind is perfectly capable of listening intelligently to a speaker and, at the same time, watching for the visible signs of speech. The difficulty is to remember to watch for them if, in the circumstances, you are hearing quite well.

Practise variations of the sounds in this and previous chapters with the following:

filth	theft
shift	loft
lathe	lush
thrill	shun
thatch	lunch
churlish	church
value	vanish

Violence in films can be very frightening.

Fashion photography visually displays the latest fantasy.

Flowers in fragile vases frequently fail to survive.

A surfeit of fattening foods fails to improve the figure.

Verify the tension first.

Her favourite little vanities.

The verger's version failed to verify the facts.

Jelly fish.

George's journey over the ocean justified his ambition.

The idea of this list that you will study them on your image in the mirror, watching the formation of the signpost shapes as they happen. If then you can find someone to read out to you the whole list, without voice, you would get some real practice (and possibly some discouragement because it is a very difficult test). Ignoring the result of the voiceless exercise, repeat it with voice, because the whole aim is to enable the reader to combine seeing and hearing. It's the two together that works when, for most of us, we have awakened our eyes to see the sound.

8   L and Dark L

Start by saying into the mirror the sounds T, D, N, L, a few times, and watch carefully. What you will see, taking it slowly, is that there is practically no difference between T and D, but there is something to see when you watch N and L; 'en' or 'and' compared with 'el'. Look at the photograph of L – the tip of the tongue travels upwards to touch the palate just behind the front top teeth. Spend a little time with the mirror saying 'el'.

The point I am making is that there is a very slight similarity between N and L. In the mirror, say 'when' and 'well' or 'When will William come?' Speak normally but fast, and then pedantically, showing the Ls. Say, 'When on earth will William come?' or better still, see if you can induce someone else to say it to you. In the mirror, say

little	liable
lovely	liability
lovable	syllable
apple	you'll see
apples	people

People say silly things

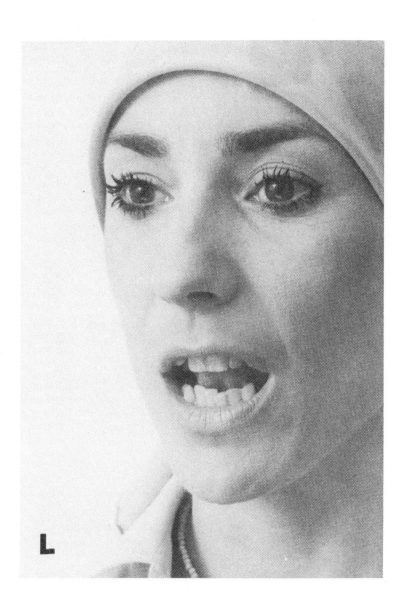

L

These are a few samples, showing there are nice visible Ls and what have been called dark Ls which escape being seen, often part of a double consonant. As a signpost L suffers from being vandalised by other sounds preceding or following it.

flat

flight

ambulance

black

lance corporals

feel the

wealth

When you are speaking, you may be unaware of the dark Ls, but you can always feel the L being made.

This may seem all rather technical but it's desirable so as to be able to tell your eyes what to look for. L is often seen if one gets a side view of the speaker. Some more L's to watch

blame

black

flute

glutton

plural

slaughter.

It can be a matter of opinion whether an L is dark, or visible. A speaker can certainly make them more visible by careful technique.

A sharp eye, an attentive ear, and an alert mind all add up to better hearing. L is not a loud sound, but it is audible: sometimes easy to see, but not always. Alertness (see this word in the mirror) of vision and mind are the key. Indeed, the word 'invisible' is not used by teachers of very good lipreaders because they always see something – either a face muscle moves, or the jaw, or a throat movement is seen. Of course it might be that their skill is now sufficient for them to be able to use their mental agility more quickly, and the teacher can never be sure what percentage of each is involved. If you have trouble with L's, try this:

Live and let live.

He laughs loudest who laughs last.

'Trouble' itself is a cause of difficulty with the L. A lipspeaker can make the dark L more visible by just taking the trouble to do so. Say 'The trouble' and then 'The trouble to do so' in the mirror. In ordinary speech the L tends to get lost unless there is a momentary break between the '–ble' and the 't–' of '. . . to do so'. Try it in the mirror and decide whether to help the lipreader, or just talk and let him work it out. It depends rather on how good a lipreader you are speaking to. With a moment's effort you can let in a little light on a dark L. Another good example is 'Wholemeal bread' compared with 'Home-made bread'. Try both in the mirror. There is only a little difference. If you cannot see the dark Ls, only the long vowel EE is the clue.

9   R and Combinations

The shape photographed is the one most usually made. It is basically described as raising the inner side of the lower lip towards the upper teeth. There is movement of the chin upwards. It needs to be studied because there is variation with different people. Of course, the Scot rolls his rrr's with his tongue but there is still something of the basic shape. It is a good shape to see. Compare it with F in the mirror.

Fat	Rat	Rot	Font
Fen	Rent	Rook	Foot
Fit	Writ	Rut	Fun

There is a difference which you should be able to see. You also want to study what happens when the R is preceded by a 'b' or 'p' – 'brother', 'proud'. Lipspeak such words to the mirror and also study what happens when other people say 'brother', 'bread', 'priest', 'friend', 'shred', 'thread'. Sometimes the 'b' of brother

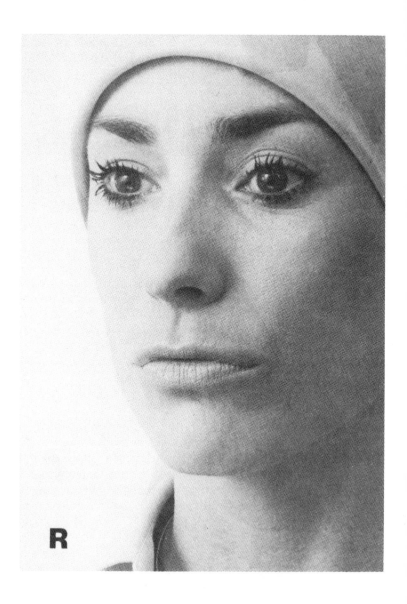
R

makes the shape change rather like an SH shape when the upper lip becomes involved. The curling of the lower lip is the characteristic of the R shape. Incidentally, 'mirror' is a good word to study. The M seems to affect the R. For the mirror:

Round the rugged rock the ragged rascal ran.

When you say 'ran', watch and you will see the N at the end as the tongue goes up while the lips are still open. 'Peter Pan' gives another visible N if your tongue moves before your lips and jaw close. Study 'pant' and 'pants'. So the 'n', 'nt', and 'nts' could be described as seeable and missable. Compare 'mother' and 'brother'.

Lipreading is a bit like playing darts. One day you are on form and another day you miss a lot. The darts player usually has a glass of beer at hand to keep his eye in. The lipreader needs plenty of confidence to help out. The darts player gets a bit of physical exercise, but the lipreader gets some intense mental exercise, usually sitting comfortably. So the lipreader's confidence is more likely to be nourished by a relaxed mental attitude and a rest at intervals.

The R may be preceded by other consonants, *e.g.* 'b', 'p', 'sh', 'th', 't', 'f', 'g', 'c', 'k', 'd', or 'p'.

rain, train, grain, crane, drain

Unfortunately, it is difficult to see the difference. It is possible to hear the difference if your hearing is acute enough and there is always the context. When someone says 'rain', the context is likely to give the vital clue to the consonant which you have not seen. 'We'll be late for the train', 'We are short of grain for the chickens', 'We must have the drains seen-to soon', 'Surely it can't go on raining much longer', 'We are overshadowed by that huge crane'. When R or W ends a word, they become part of the preceding vowel, and do not make any separate sound either visually or audibly. Examples: 'pillow', 'hollow', 'tomorrow', 'few', 'new', 'tar', 'war', 'poor', 'fur', 'for'. If the word ending with R or W is followed by a word beginning with the same sound – 'a new word' – or by a vowel – 'a rare art' – that's different. It all means you must watch out!

10   W and Q

The W shape is rather, but not quite, like the OO vowel shape. WH is visually almost the same as W.

> When do you want your breakfast?

In English there is no W shape at the end of a word. In words like 'pillow', 'chew', 'new', and 'draw', the W becomes part of the vowel shape.

> A new word.

> Waste not, want not.

> I don't owe you anything.

A sentence beginning with a W may often be a question: 'What . . . ?'   'Where . . . ?'   'Which . . . ?'   'When . . . ?' 'Why . . . ?' The context and facial expression may be a clue.

Q and W have to be studied together. The difference between them will seldom if ever be detectable by sight alone. 'Query' and 'weary' look exactly the same. 'Quite' and 'quick' look like 'white' and 'wick'. 'Queen' looks like 'wean' and 'well' may be 'quell'. 'Quandary' could be lipread as 'wandering' but would not make sense. The W is rather nice and easy to see, but I find it takes time to remember to become suspicious if the W makes a word that doesn't fit the sentence. My masterpiece of stupidity was once when royalty was the subject, and I lipread the word 'wean' which did not make sense, and my mind searched for a W word which would. I quite forgot about the Queen!

You would be very lucky if you ever saw the difference between the KW which makes a Q and W. There always may be something which somebody can see: perhaps a faint delay before the W or perhaps a tiny movement in the throat.

'Write' and 'wrong' show that lipreading is only concerned with the phonetics or the actual sound, and not the spelling. It is quite possible that as one becomes more efficient at lipreading, the ability to spell correctly may deteriorate.

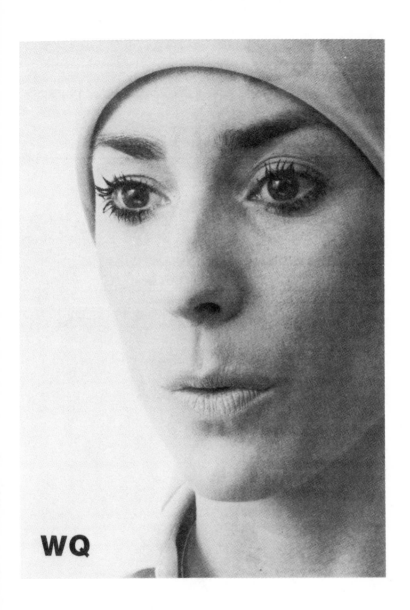

Finally some more banana skins of which to beware:

quire – wire	quake – wake
quill – will	quad – wad
quest – west	quip – whip
quench – wench	quirk – work
quaver – waver	quart – wart
quarter – water	query – weary

I had a good example in the class recently of the advantages and disadvantages of the analytic and synthetic methods (see p. 12), in relation to lipreading the Q/W shape. We had been reading, without voice, about a roof which needed various repairs. Then came a description of what happened when it rained and men had to come. The voiceless words were, 'They went up on to the roof quickly and made a repair.' I must have been applying the mental anticipation of the synthetic method, because I lipread, inaccurately, that the men went up on the roof *willingly* (in the rain!). When you analyse my mistake, it was not important, but it was interesting how I got over the – to me – invisible Q. I found a suitable word beginning with W which did have two 'l's when 'quickly' has only one. Note that the most visible shapes were the W and the 'ly'. So I got 'wi' and 'ly' and I only cheated by putting two syllables where one had been lipspoken. It could be said that I got the gist of the meaning of the sentence.

11   S, X and Z

There is no photograph of the S shape which is also the X, the Z shape and the soft C shape. I did not photograph it because there is quite a variety of shapes that different people make. Back to the mirror. See what shape you make for S.

Sister Susie's sewing shirts for soldiers

Sing a song of sixpence

Then try to observe what other people do. The ideal shape is when the upper and lower teeth are nearly closed and visible. But sometimes all there is to see is a slight movement in the corners of the mouth.

The X is really 'ecks' but the 'ck' comes among the not very visibles (p. 36). As a rule, X lipreads as S – 'extraordinary', 'excuse', 'exam'. Therefore, a little caution must be attached to S. It may be X, like W may be Q. Sometimes S is pronounced Z, as in 'observe'. It is not always easy to see whether a word is singular or plural because the S gets lost at the end of the word. Also it can be difficult if there are too many S sounds, as in the word 'soliciting', or 'solicitous'. There is very little to see, even if the L is shown clearly, except a slight rapid movement of the jaw. With the help of context and practice, the word may become lipreadable as a whole: 'He had a legal problem and consulted his solicitor.' Try it in the mirror, but never forget that you could solicit a friend to come and lipspeak to you and share the mirror.

12   Double Vowels

The long vowels were illustrated in Chapter 5 – (AH, OR/AW, OO, EE and ER). These cover a large number of vowel sounds with a variety of spellings. If you turn back to that chapter and remind yourself of what you saw in the mirror and the respective shapes, it will help now when we study what can be called the double vowels. They are OI as in 'boy' or 'oil', OU as in 'out' or 'cow', EA as in 'ear', 'deer' and 'dear' and I as in 'eye' or 'I' (the first person singular).

The important thing about these double vowels is that there is a sliding motion of the shapes as they move from one shape to the other. Now you need the mirror. The one I like best is 'boy'. Say it in the mirror.

Come here, boy.

Boys and girls.

It is almost impossible to cut the sliding movement, however sharply you say 'boy'. The vowel in 'boy' is a double one and the vowel in 'girl' is the long vowel ER.

Next the OU as in 'sound' or 'out': again you see the sliding shapes, even when speaking sharply. 'Out, damned spot.' Now 'ear': once more the sliding movement which makes it impossible to photograph EA in a still photo. But you can see it in speech and you can give it just that little help in lipspeaking.

Then there is 'eye'.

My eyesight improves with spectacles.

I deny fighting for my rights.

You can see the sliding movement in the mirror. Don't forget the possibility of studying these things on the lips of someone else if you can arrange it. It helps to watch other lips. O as in 'owe' or 'home' or 'dole' or 'Oh, no don't', has got the sliding movement. Try it in the mirror. The great thing is to be able to recognise it in speech together with the context. It is a bit like the OR/AW shape except for the 'o' closing towards the 'w' shape. Likewise there is the A shape as in 'aim'. This is a sliding shape, as though there were a little 'i' after the basic 'a' shape. 'A', 'K', 'pay','cave', 'David', 'amazing', 'name', 'fade'.

For mirror practice, say 'David' and 'darling' – that compares the AH single long vowel with the sliding 'a' shape. More words to compare:

pavement	pipework
maintain	martyr
fool	fated painter
fade	farmer

You have to watch your image in the mirror carefully to see the slight difference. That is why lipreading needs practice and practice. So does your friend, if only to lipspeak. It is possible to regard the O shape as a long vowel plus a short vowel, 'Ooo' or 'owe', the 'oo' being the short vowel in 'good', 'put'. In the same way, the 'A' shape could be 'Ai'.

Mirror practice for Ooo and Ai (and some others): Today, toad, dough, day, throw, hay, mow, may, moat, mate, more, mart, most, murder, Mayday, Pope, pauper, payday, tool, toilet, feel, date.

The complete set of double vowels involving sliding motion is:

OI   boy, oil, royal, foil, noise, ahoy, toy.

EA   ear, hear, rear, sphere, mere, steer, career.

OU   out, flout, tout, sprout, count, mount.

AI   air, care, where, share, hair, hare.

A   day, say, they, eight, rate, mate.

I   eye, my, sky, flight, might.

O   owe, no, don't, moat, float, joke.

U   ewe, new, due, few, huge, Hugh.

OOR   dour, lour.

The vowels of the alphabet appear again in the last four, and yet again in the next chapter on short vowels. It is useful to know about these things, but obviously you cannot analyse every vowel as you lipread, any more than you do when reading printed words. For the mirror:

The aim of either boy is to throw it out.

The heir to the throne travelled by air.

pear	pair	
pare	mare	
fare	bear	(Remember PBM?)
bear	bare	

It is useful to compare the words 'heart' and 'height' the long vowel AH with the double vowel I or EI. Try them in the mirror. You can say them with little difference, but you should show a slight widening of the lip shape with the sliding movement, for 'height'. It is important for both lipreaders and speakers. The difference demands sharp observation by the lipreader, and careful speech.

The double vowel is really a mixture of two vowels, long or short, or perhaps short and short. For lipreaders it is not necessary to delve too deeply – leave that to the speech therapists – it is enough to know they exist and can be seen.

13 Short Vowels, Neutral Vowels and Accents

There is, of course, a vowel in every word. I have often thought that in the very first class one went to, or the very first time one saw a silent word on someone's lips, one recognised the vowel instinctively. It might have been a long vowel, a double vowel, or a short one. The complete concentration on someone's lips probably revives long-lost memories from our infancy and we are not actually surprised that we lipread the word or words. Lipreading, which is concerned with sounds, not spelling, has five long vowels, six short vowels and nine double vowels. Together with a neutral vowel, this makes twenty-one vowels in all. The five vowels of the alphabet represent twenty-one different sounds!

I like to divide short vowels into two sets of three. The first three are a bit difficult to distinguish from each other by sight. Back to the mirror again.

Pat   pet   pit

Say them into the mirror. There is a little difference, but not much to see. The best thing to do with them is to class them as 'guessables' and move on to the next three.

Pot   put   putt

These are more visible. Study them carefully in the mirror. It is interesting – they happen to be a, e, i, o and two u's!

The short vowels occur often in speech. I have seen them described as the little offspring of the long ones, or something like that. There is some truth in it. Try making a comparison in the mirror. Say 'pot' and then 'port', or try 'put' and 'port'. Compare 'put' and 'pert'. Remind yourself of the long vowels AW and ER. Try 'put' and 'who' (long vowel OO). Then 'hood' and 'who'. It does not matter whether you see a family resemblance in the shapes, as long as you get the idea. It is all helping the eyes to see sounds rapidly, as they do when reading the printed word. Thinking back, one has been lipreading short vowels without knowing it, in the course of studying the long ones, consonants, etc. Some short vowels crop up in almost anything you say. Again it makes me wonder whether we have all noticed much more about the visible appearance of speech than we consciously realise.

Studying words with the sounds of the short vowels is helpful, and I have found it useful to commit to memory the six similar words containing the six short vowels:

a	e	i	o	u	u
pat	pet	pit	pot	put	putt
at	end	it	hot	good	under
sad	said	is	dog	should	undo
thank	dead	isn't it	cough	could	jungle
McAdam	head	ink	trough	wood	rough

For those who have some hearing, with or without hearing aid, the 'pat', 'pet', 'pit' ones are easy to hear and not so easy to see, but the 'pot', 'put' and 'putt' ones are easy to hear and a bit easier to see.

Previously (p. 12) I have referred to the analytic method of lipreading when we have a single word to see, without context or clue. Then the mind has to break down the word into consonant, vowel (long or short), etc. This would be appropriate with short vowels when you have seen the shape of, say, either 'hot', 'hood' or 'hut' and recognised it. The word 'dog' has the short vowel 'o', like 'hot'. Watch your image saying 'Hot dog'. There is a difference to see but it is pretty difficult. So with 'good' or 'gut', especially without context or clue. The analytical recognition of these vowels might help with a context, but if the short vowel is not recognised and there is no context, there is, lipreading-wise, almost no word. So the best thing to do is to ignore it and go to the next and the next, in the hope that something will give a clue. This is the synthetic or rhythmic method.

Neutral vowels are found in: mother, father, sister, banana, enemy. A whole word may become neutral depending on stress, for example: cup *of* tea, bunch *of* flowers. So the neutral vowel plays a very important part in our language – it gives us rhythm. In French, for example, all vowels carry equal weight. Watch as you say 'bunch of flowers' giving each word equal stress. Now say it naturally – can you see the difference?

51

Effect of Accents on vowels

With all vowels, accent affects the shape. Remember the old song: 'You say tomatoes and I say tomatoes'? (tom ah toes / toe may toes). Another example – someone with a West Country accent may pronounce the word 'bath' with a short vowel 'a' where a Southerner may say 'bath' with the long 'ah'. When coming across someone with an accent for the first time, it can throw you but, once you realise they *have* an accent, you can readily 'slot' in to it and you will soon be lipreading in that accent. When you become a practised lipreader you will begin to tell straight away that someone is talking to you with an accent. One of the great advantages of being a lipreader (and there are many) is that you may well be able to tell where someone comes from just by watching them speak.

14   Lipspeaking

You need to be relaxed to lipspeak. It is a strain if the lipreader cannot read you, but you must keep calm and never try to 'mouth' in an attempt to help. Only the slightest exaggeration is readable. Keep the rhythm, slow down a little, repeat a few times. Then, if necessary, stop and speak with voice, or write it. Whenever you speak, remember someone listening may not hear too well. Even unaffected ears will hear all the better if you lipspeak with voice.

Some other rather obvious lipspeaking rules: Get the attention of the person lipreading. Look at the person before you start. When you begin, remember to feel your lips working and your mouth moving. But don't 'mouth' words, don't exaggerate more than a trifle but pronounce every syllable. Don't fidget, don't move your head about, or wave your arms or put your hand in front of your mouth. Don't smile because it will change the shapes. See that your face is in a good light.

One day in class, the teacher asked each of us a question without voice. Without thinking, I answered without voice. There was an embarrassing moment for both of us until I repeated my reply out loud. That started me seriously to think whether my voiceless talk was lipreadable. Indeed, I am still thinking. It is one thing to see your image in the mirror making all the right shapes, and another to remember to *feel* yourself making the shapes clearly when speaking to someone.

It is good training to think what you are saying, and feel yourself making the lipshapes as you speak. Talking to another lipreading student, there are several things to be conscious of at the same time: Is he hearing you? Is he good at lipreading? Can you phrase it better? Are you lipspeaking properly? It is dead easy to lipread your image in the mirror because you know what it is saying. Only trial and error will tell you whether you lipspeak properly, readably to other people. Anyone who has made a serious attempt to master the lipshapes illustrated should be easier to lipread than most hearing people talking colloquially.

An example might be the word 'curtain'. Most people would say it as one syllable – 'curtn'. Say it to your image in the mirror and feel how you make the 'tn' sound – the tongue comes up behind the front teeth closing the mouth (not the lips) and air is blown down the nose from the back. Now say the word 'curt' and note the difference. Now say the word 'colonel' or 'kernel', followed by 'earn' or 'urn'. The 'n' is the nasal one. In 'turn', the 't' actually needs some outgoing breath. So to say the word correctly, as distinct from the way you might normally, 'curtain' is two syllables – 'cur t–n'. Say one after the other 'curn', 'curt', 'cur t–n', 'kernel', 'urn', 'turn'. Note what you can see and what you can hear. 'The colonel asked him to draw the curtains, turn on the light and earn his thanks.' Note how helpful a bit of context can be.

Lipspeaking does also require mental agility. If you can see that what you say is not being lipread, the thing to do is to rephrase it, using words with easy lipshapes if you can think of some quickly. A phrase with a number of words, or a sentence, spoken at even a normal speed, leaves a lipreader little time to operate with mental agility in return. A basic skill in lipspeaking is to slow down enough to help the lipreader's problems, without losing the rhythm of a sentence. The human mind tends to anticipate that a conversation will run upon the same lines unless warned of a change. For instance, if the subject has been domestic chores and you suddenly change it by asking, 'Do you like watching sport?' you may get a good laugh if your lipreader replies, 'No, I don't like washing smalls.' There's very little difference between 'sport' and 'smalls'. Try them in the mirror.

When you speak to a lipreader, always make sure, by any means available, that the first few words, indicating the general subject, have been understood. This applies to voiceless speaking in particular.

The lipreader has to work hard trying to read all the 'ventriloquists' met in daily life, so deserves a little help when you know how to lipspeak. Never overdo it. In spite of all temptations, keep the rhythm, speak a bit slower and clearer. The television, whenever you see a good view of the speaker's face, is an excellent source of practice for lipreading and lipspeaking. Take one of the illustrated shapes and watch for it. You can do this as well as following the programme.

Notice those speakers who show clear shapes, have mobile lips, and speak so well that you can listen to every word and lipread quite a lot. Notice the ones who speak through their teeth with little movement and then, of course, the 'ventriloquists' who rarely part their lips at all. It is always good practice listening to the meaning of what is being said and watching what it looks like at the same time. The day may come when, reading voiceless speech successfully, you get an uncanny feeling as though you had heard it.

15   The 'Loop' System

The 'loop' system is being installed in some theatres, churches and halls to help those with suitable hearing aids. It is also possible to have it in the home. The basic principle, in non-technical terms, is that a hearing aid with the switch at the 'T' position will receive sound from a wire surrounding an area. The wire comes from an amplifier, goes round the area, and back to the same amplifier which has received the sound from a television or radio, or from microphone(s) on the stage, pulpit or platform. Some railway booking office windows have a loop fitted to enable the ticket clerk to communicate with anyone who has a hearing aid on the 'T' switch.

I have a set consisting of an amplifier, a microphone, and

enough wire to go right round a large room. The wire is fitted into the amplifier which has volume control. The microphone is connected to the amplifier, and is then placed close to the speaker on either radio or TV. The result of using the loop is that others in the room may have the volume of sound from the radio or TV lower than the volume desired by those with hearing loss. At the same time I – and anyone else in the same room with a hearing aid on the 'T' switch – can regulate the volume of sound in the loop by the amplifier, and also by the hearing aid itself. The quality of the sound, of speech in particular, is very much clarified through the 'loop' compared with what I get through the hearing aid alone.

Using the 'loop' in an ordinary room, I have found that the volume setting for sound from the television should not be very low. If it is, the 'loop' microphone and amplifier are not getting the best sound to work on. Of course, the volume needed will be affected by what is being broadcast. I and most others with hearing loss abhor the programmes which delight in using the full range of sound – one moment there is hardly anything to hear, and the next one's eardrum is in danger. Therefore I advocate experiment to decide on a comfortable volume of sound. You may get an irritating sound which is not intended, together with the broadcast programme. It's the sort of sound you will hear if, with your hearing aid on 'T' switch, you put your head very close to the TV set when it is switched on. If you then switch your hearing aid to the 'M' or 'on' position, the noise vanishes. I have had it with the news reader, when it came and went exactly as his image came and went. The cure may be to increase the volume by the amplifier and reduce it by the hearing aid control. It may be to tune the television more accurately. By experiment, the right balance is soon found.

There is a practical problem resulting from frequent use of the 'T' switch and the volume control of the hearing aid. Forgetting to readjust them for normal use is terribly easy. When it is left on the 'T' switch, it is the equivalent of 'off' for anything but the 'loop'. I have often had a sensation that my hearing has taken a turn for the worse until I remember. I have learned that when my own voice sounds a bit peculiar to me, it is probably the 'T' switch left on, the volume too low or the battery run down.

The microphone, amplifier and 'loop' can also be used for conversation with hearing aid on 'T' switch. This will probably involve planning positions for the microphone and those taking part within the area of the 'loop'. The first time I heard a speaker through a 'loop' at a meeting, I was most impressed because it was just as if he was speaking into my ear from close by. Every syllable was quite clear. A strange experience followed when he asked for questions and someone from the back of the audience spoke without a microphone. I could hear him speak, but not what he said, so I turned round to see him and the moment I saw him I could hear what he was saying. It was a rewarding example of how sight and lipreading promptly acted as a hearing aid. Mine would have been still on the 'T' switch.

Because forgetting to return the volume control back to normal after using the 'loop' is so easy, I would recommend a look at p. 59, where I have described making marks to show the normal position. It is most convenient to be able to set the volume at about normal and make slight variations according to conditions.

There are one or two other kinds of interference you should know about. If you have fluorescent tube lights, you may hear them. When your TV is on but the sound right down, if you are near enough you will hear a mains noise. Check that this is not audible from where you normally sit. You can also hear it through a wall in your own house, or through the semi-detached wall from your neighbour. In a block of flats or terraced houses, a 'loop' may be audible through a wall, floor or ceiling. If that should occur from your or your neighbour's 'loop', some neighbourly diplomacy may be wise.

The amplifier I have for the 'loop' has an Automatic Gain Control (AGC). If the volume setting of the TV is too low, or the microphone is too far from the loudspeaker, the AGC operates and might cause mains hum to be heard. The remedy is easy. Make sure the microphone is close to the loudspeaker of the TV. Mine is suspended, touching the loudspeaker grill.

My TV set has a push-button AFC (automatic frequency control), which locks the tuning on to the channel selected. I have been told that owing to the need to keep down the price of TV sets, it may not be entirely accurate. This might mean some slight retuning. However, I have found my remedy by reducing the volume by the hearing aid volume control satisfactory on rare occasions when there is interference.

Of course, one good reason for attending a class, or joining a club, is that there may be someone with a loop system willing to invite you to hear it.

Warning: When you are *alone* listening via the loop,. with your hearing aid on T, you may be *deaf* to telephone or front door bells, and very unpopular with the caller! Ask about solutions to the problem at your hearing aid centre.

16   Final Thoughts

Through the Looking Glass (with apologies to Lewis Carroll): ' "How can I hear you if you don't speak up?" roared the Queen at Alice.' ' "She should *hear* what she *can* and *see* what she *can't*," said the Cheshire Cat and promptly vanished.'

It takes a cat to sum it all up in so few words. So let us look back into the looking glass, lipspeaker, lipreader and all.

It takes time to acquire a habit, good or bad. The good habit you must get is to look whenever you listen. The brain can cope easily with seeing and listening together. I will never forget seeing a church organist playing the music with his hands and feet, pushing and pulling the stops while he carried on a conversation with someone beside him. We can concentrate on both the sound and sight of speech, get the meaning and agree or disagree with it, all at once. The twelve lipshapes illustrated are the easiest to see and recognise as they form momentarily during speech, and must be learned.

As children, we all went through it to learn the alphabet and then to read. With practice, we learned to see groups of letters as words at a glance, even long words, or several words. First, we had to know the letters. The printed word stays put on the paper. The lipshaped words are in constant movement, together with the sound. The advantage we have over the child is that we already know the language. Very few, if any, of us have never noticed something of what speech looks like.

If you have the strength of will, go back to the twelve shapes, one at a time, and see if you can, during a period of days, concentrate on each whenever you see anyone speaking. A good way to get practice is with the television when you can see the speaker's face well. Reduce the volume of sound to a point when you can only just hear it. Alternatively, turn off your hearing aid. I think, under such conditions, the memory of lipshapes learned is stimulated and sight begins to assist the sound. The P, B and M shape (lips closed) becomes more noticeable. The F and V shape seems easier to see and the same with the SH and various others, even with rapid speech.

You will be your own taskmaster. If you find both master and pupil are none too diligent, don't give up too soon. Remember the mirror. Here is one to think about. The long vowel OO and the consonant W (QU): the photographs do show the difference – just. Practice them in the mirror. 'Two hooligans went away.' 'What do you want?' 'The wet winter was quite wonderful for the flowers'. 'Who has won?' 'One, two.'

From now on you have to invent your own exercises and lipreading problems. See if you can remember the five long vowels and seven consonant shapes. Every time you think about them, see them on your image's face or other people's, and you are one degree nearer the day when you cannot quite hear until you can see the speakers. It is a great day. Remember you learn more from other people's lips than from your own. Still more from attending a class with a qualified teacher, where you will meet others like yourself, even some who are profoundly deaf.

One last thought, any loss of hearing can contribute to turning a normal human being into a 'loner' who opts out. All the time things are happening to help us to opt in. 'Loop' systems steadily increase in theatres and meeting places. More and more hearing people are learning what the hearing-impaired need to make life easier: the scientists are working all the time to improve our lot. Watch out for all these things. Laugh and the world laughs with you, weep and you weep alone.

Appendix

Hearing Aids

Anyone for whom it is a problem to hear just what is said, should go to their own doctor and tell him all the facts. He will probably send you to a hospital for an audiometric test. There may be waiting lists, so it would be wise not to delay. It takes a bit of time getting used to the hearing aid, putting it in, taking it out, working the little wheel controlling the volume. If in any way you and the hearing aid do not get on well with each other, do go straight back to the hearing aid centre. If you think wearing it will be horribly obvious to everyone, don't worry: if they do notice it, the reaction is generally quite pleasant. Remember that with the aid in one ear, you have some loss of ability to judge the direction from which sound is coming. You must use your eyes even more in traffic.

In my experience, one is occasionally faced with more or less insoluble questions. Is it the hearing aid? A bad recording? Is the television or radio too loud or too soft? Is someone speaking too loudly, too softly or just too quickly? Is my ear affected by excess wax? Sometimes you may ask a companion watching television with you, 'Could you hear what that person was saying?' And the answer you get will leave you wondering whether it meant, 'Yes' or 'No' or 'I wasn't really listening.'

The hearing aid I have has a switch marked

O
T
M

The O stands for OFF, the T stands for TELEPHONE, the M for MICROPHONE or ON. Above these is the compartment for the battery and above that the small wheel with no markings. If you turn the little wheel one way, it increases the volume of sound and the other way reduces the sound. You will find it a great help to learn which way is which when you have the aid in place behind your ear. Also, it is well worth while to make a mark on the wheel and one on the body of the instrument so that you can set it at a position suited to you, before putting it on. The position of the mark is best found by trial and error: what is comfortable when having a conversation, or listening to TV or radio. I used Indian ink and an old fashioned dip pen and a steady hand. Make one dot on the wheel and another dot beside it. Ordinary ink does not last but can be renewed.

Often members of the family and friends are the first to recognise the symptoms of hearing loss, not the sufferer. It is a terrible temptation, until the fact of personal hearing loss has become known to the sufferer, for the family to try to ignore it and 'get by'. This can only be done at the cost of irritation when trying to converse. For the sake of harmony in the home it is important somebody should do something about it. We are all loathe to admit the ravages of age.

It does seem that the hearing aid which helps with speech does not work so well with music. We used to enjoy concerts and music, quite modern works too, but they do not come over now the way they used to, on radio, etc. The hearing aid provided for people like me, who have a hearing loss in the high frequency range of sounds (like the tick of my pendulum referred to on p. 7) will find that the sound of the piano has become unpleasantly 'metallic' or 'tinny'. If we listen without the hearing aid, the sound of the piano is much more mellow, but the volume may need an increase with TV and radio, which may be unpopular with the neighbours. Even so, we soon feel there is something missing in the treble. The high frequencies are boosted by the hearing aid which makes speech intelligible, but unfortunately the same boost makes singers 'squawky', the piano 'tinny' and music not at all what it used to be. That, sad to say, is that.

Ear Wax

Nature produces wax in the channel or canal in the outer ear (from outside to the ear drum). Unfortunately, this may be produced or collect in excess. The remedy is to see the doctor. He will give or prescribe treatment which may be to apply drops for a few days and then have the channel syringed. Normally this is quite effective and harmless. Do not imagine that you can solve the problem by yourself. For instance, many people have thought that the wax could be extracted by carefully removing it using some small instrument. In most households a pin may be readily found. If you touch the ear drum with the pin, it will feel the same as the channel, but it is only a thin piece of skin, easily perforated, with appalling consequences.

Useful Addresses

The Association of Teachers of Lipreading to Adults (ATLA)

The Secretary
The Police Cottage
Green Road
Wivelsfield Green
Sussex RH17 7QP
(Tel: 0444 84257)

The Information Officer
The Post Office
Slimbridge
Gloucestershire GL2 7BL

(The Secretary is in office from 1986 for three years. The new Secretary's address may be obtained from the RNID or the City Lit – addresses below – or write to the ATLA Information Officer at the address above.)

Age Concern

Bernard Sunley House, Pitcairn Road, Mitcham, Surrey, CR4 3LL
(Tel: 01 640 5431)   (See also local telephone book)

Royal National Institute for the Deaf (RNID)

105 Gower Street, London WC1E 6AH
(Tel: 01 387 8033)

British Association for the Hard of Hearing (BAHOH)

7–11 Armstrong Road, Acton, London, W3 7JL
(Tel: 01 743 1110)

Their magazine HARK published quarterly

City Lit

Keely House, Keely Street, London, WC2B 4BA
(Tel: 02 430 0548)

The Adult Education Department

Local authority concerned

The Hearing Aid Centre, DHSS

Local hospital

The Sympathetic Hearing Scheme

7–11 Armstrong Road, London, W3 7JL
(Tel: 01 843 1110)

The Local Public Library

The Link Centre for Deafened People

19 Hartfield Road, Eastbourne, BN21 2AR
(Tel: 0323 638 230)